SERGIUS
SEEKS
BACCHUS

TRANSLATED BY

SERGIUS SEEKS BACCHUS

NORMAN ERIKSON PASARIBU

TIFFANY TSAO

TILTED AXIS PRESS

Langit-langit

In Indonesian, you repeat a word to pluralise it. But in colloquial speech, repetition can also be used to minimise a term, turning it into a toy or imitation: 'kuda' is a horse, 'kuda-kudaan' is a toy wooden horse. 'Langit' is the sky, the sight of a borderless world, heaven. 'Langit-langit' is the ceiling, the wall above, the fake sky. In this book, 'Langit' is the name of a future child of a male couple, the hint of liberation, the start of a new era. But it has to start from a leak in the ceiling, a car in an underground car park, a suffocating interiority, before taking a leap of faith to depart for the outside, to bask in the light of day.

'You are home now, outsider, for what that's worth.'

Gregory Pardlo, *Digest*

'Meanwhile, we lose our sense of wonder.
The world is no longer mysterious.'

Jack Cohen, *Major Philosophers of
Jewish Prayer in the Twentieth Century*

FOR LEO,
who too fell in love with footnote to howl

ERRATUM

What was he thinking here, picking this body
and this family, where being match-made
with your mother's niece was possible,
where first-born sons always meant everything,
and here, falling in love with the boy
who sat beside him at school,
when all that lingered of first love was that first kiss
they shared when cutting PE,
and here, not long after his first book came out,
as his family sat cross-legged together and ate,
he told them it wouldn't end with any girl,
much less the Toba or Karo kind,
and here as he stood by the side of the road
that night, all alone, cars passing him,
his father's words hounding him,
Don't ever come back, Banci,
and he wept under a streetlight, frightened
at the first drops of rain misting his hair,
and here when he realised something odd about the
text that was his life and hoped sometime soon
the Publisher would print an erratum
to restore the lost lines, wherein
he'd know he was everything and also nothing
was wrong with him, and he'd know
what lingered of first love
was that very first kiss, bestowed
back when his family sat cross-legged together
and ate, grateful because he had picked
this body and this family?

LOVE

When the rain pays a visit
and he's sitting at home,
he climbs up the stairs and into this room
to make sure there are no leaks
between the ceiling and the sky.

HE AND THE TREE

At high noon he sought forgiveness from the solitary tree
at the edge of the company parking lot, where it sheltered his car
from the sun. He sought forgiveness for his granddad, the palm oil
company's founder, for the whole clan, really, who'd spent
generations taking a carpenter for god's own son. The tree sobbed,
recalling suddenly his childhood friend who had been ripped
from the earth for being 'too close to the foundation'.
From afar they used to exchange mischievous glances and winks
and daydream about growing up, when birds and butterflies would alight
on their branches and leaf buds to help them pass notes back and forth.
The tree regretted not telling his friend that he loved him.
If he were here, he would take him to a church. At the altar
they would be joined together before god, who had three branches
—like a tree—and their children would fill the lot, every
single square inch, so that someday everyone who passed
would think a forest had sprung up in the city's heart.
The man hugged the tree and the tree hugged the man.

Snake-like, you shed your short-lived skin
and commence/continue your quest. Now the light from on high

passes through you. You're luminous. Meanwhile, out west
in decrepit Rome sits Galerius, oblivious his end is nigh.

You seek your beloved—he appeared to you in your cell,
his body glowing silver as he whispered, *Endure,*

for I will always watch over you. With him you'll rise
up to heaven and wonder at how familiar

it all feels. Hand in hand, you two will stroll the streets,
introducing one another to everyone you meet.

Laos dilanglangi do ahu, tarlungun-lungun…
(In the places I wander, my heart weeps…)

—from the Batak pop song, *Mardalan Ahu*

Time to turn in the resignation letter
you've been dying to write for so long. Time
to reveal all the credit card statements. Time
to come clean to your wife. Time
to confess it was never the work meetings
that were sapping you of strength.

This whole time, loneliness has been your leafage,
green and shaggy and lush. What a fine tree, they all think,
on the verge of buzzing with bees and bursting with fruit.
But you're withering,
your trunk and twigs diminishing, the benalu
in your branches eating away at your heart.

Time to stop living a lie. Everything is
nothing but a show. And you're a bad actor
with no script, trying to make her life your stage.
Who's watching? Your folks—and empty seats.
You stand in the spotlight, unfiltered, unpink,
performing an endless series of bad tricks.

At first, you'd wake up in the middle of the night,
haunted by how your life had turned out: racking up bills
in cheap hotels and the unripe tang of cum in your throat.
Then you heard your name murmured in sleep.
So she really does love me.
You shut yourself in the bathroom and wept.

This morning, you and she reached your golden years at last,
straggling as the alang-alang sprouting in the yard
behind where you grew up, playing tag with pups
to the honey melody of your Inong's psalms.
From the sofa you hear your wife crooning in the kitchen:
Laos dilanglangi do ahu, tarlungun-lungun...

You turn.

Time to tell what has transpired in the dark.
Time to gesture toward what remains.

ON THE GLORY THAT IS POETRY

Shortly before his passing
and soon after he had a vision
in which Christ revealed his hidden
mysteries, Aquinas stopped working.
To his secretary he said,
'Everything that I have written
seems to me as straw!
Nothing more than worthless straw!'
His *Summa Theologiae* was abandoned,
left unfinished, and yet
to this very day we revere it
and refer to its insights
on philosophy, theology, christology
and consider it one of the best books
written by a mere son of man.

COOKING INSTANT NOODLES
AT THE END OF THE RAINBOW

Red, yellow, green
Set in a sky of blue.
What a Glorious Painter! Who could he be?

—from the children's song, *Rainbow,* by A.T. Mahmud

Wake up at four a.m. to a cell-phone alarm ringing.
It's for Christy—her morning Quiet Time. Turn off the alarm

and make the bed. This is usually Christy's job.
Go to the kitchen and get out two packs of instant noodles. This

is usually your job.
Bring water to a boil in two small pots. Break open

the seasoning, then the chilli powder. Christy
hates spicy food while you're the reverse.

Plop the noodles in pot one and the seasoning in pot two.
Christy can't stand starchy broth and

ever considerate, you comply.
We can afford the gas, she says.

Drain the noodles in a strainer. Divide
them between two Hello Kitty bowls.

Christy bought them 'cause they were cute.
She said she wanted to be buried cute—

in pink ribbons, foundation, a little powder,
blush, mascara, and a frilly dress.

Bring both bowls into the bedroom. Savour them
alone. Christy's gone. They found her body

underneath a bridge. She'd been saying she missed
the taste of her mother's sayur lodeh.

You don't. You miss Christy. The other day
she came to you in a dream. She said:

there's nothing at the end of the rainbow.

It isn't even a painting—

just a trick of the light.

Christy—who once told you, *I'll keep pounding
on Heaven's door. Who knows? It might open*—forgot

we are all droplets of water.
We will fall to the ground but not yet.

And love is the Light!
And Love is the light!

WHAT THE DEAD ASK
FROM THE DEPARTED

(So how did we get here, pariban?)

You refused to come home in a cab with me
because you wanted to stay out and have fun.

That guy, the parlente one, bought us G&Ts and surprisingly
he listened, shared stories about his own parents, and like a nice boy

didn't hustle you into a toilet stall. On the dance floor
you two were like old friends. Later in the men's room

you gazed into the mirror and said you wanted to spend the night
with him and I said there was a exam tomorrow, and you laughed—

(I laughed?)

I think it amused you—how I could think good grades
were more important than finding the one guy

who didn't change the subject when you told him of the hours
spent seeing a shrink, and the lies you told your parents:

that you've changed, you're cured, you're brand new,
even though you stay the same, even to me, who knows you—

always as that awkward teenager, that wannabe poet
who can't write anything but depressing poems.

(Then what?)

You began skipping class. You were never in your kos.
I remember thinking, Is this happiness? Leaving everything

for someone? But one night you showed up sobbing, *I caught
something from him*, your neck swollen, teeming with blisters

like a piece of barbari bread.

Your face was so pale, like a bean sprout germinating in darkness,
so perfect. You vanished again some days later and I didn't

try to find you. Just before Christmas I heard you were dead:
the blood from your wrists flooded your parents' bathroom floor.

   (You didn't try to find me?)

Did you ever try finding *me*? Student life nibbled me up,
prevented me from living. My father found out and stopped

sending me money. I tutored rich kids everyday
so I could afford food, I moved to a cheaper kos,

where everybody shared one toilet. What can I say?
I had to save my own skin first. But once I had fled

far from the abyss I lost sight of your trail.
It was swept away by strangers shuffling by.

what do you seek in this dark pit

apart from your tears and chattering teeth

here you are with your baby face

you're empty, there's nothing to you at all

here you are yelling VIRGIL! VIRGIL!

here you are in the prime of your life

lost in the maze of your innocence, yet you want

to search for a way to grow old. You want

to reach an age where the world won't be mysterious:

(1) not to need someone to understand you

because you will finally understand yourself

(2) not to long anymore to be loved

because you will finally love yourself

you want to stop reaching for what lies beyond

no more drowning in the water of life

and expect less, life won't last forever—

you get it, poetry is only beautiful in books

and the Heaven they talk about is out of reach

in poems that never talk about you

His father was sure this was what he deserved
                              after all that He had done

—all those mistakes, those obscene acts, those sins
                              He still couldn't help but love the man

even after all he had suffered
                              feelings are such a labyrinth!

he was still sure of His life to come,
                              God would know he wasn't to blame

as was promised by the knowledge in the trees
                              he was following directions, taking cues

he could decode all the hieroglyphs about Himself
                              they were carved into every cell in his being

PARADISO

See him   here,
with   all
The Lost   &   the lives
                      never His.

UPDATE ON THE LEFT-BEHIND WOMAN

Every time they returned to their rented room after nearly
twelve hours of working non-stop, their body would demand
a bar of white chocolate.

They always wondered why this was. If their body felt hungry,
shouldn't it whip up a meal, something hearty and healthy,
and not munch instead on something so fattening, and not even
real chocolate, just emulsified sugar and milk? And if their body
couldn't be bothered to budge again, couldn't they order take-out
from the Chinese restaurant nearby, for hadn't they moved there
specifically to be in the midst of it all, the hustle and bustle, close
to practically everything their body could need—including its
favourite beauty salon, café, and dental clinic—and furthermore,
they knew perfectly well that their body had the hots for the body
of one of the delivery guys at the Chinese restaurant, dreamy,
with glasses and tousled hair, and did a body need reminding that
the restaurant had three delivery guys and therefore, the odds
of their body seeing their body's favourite body was one in three
and everybody knows that something that has a one in three chance
of happening is something that's certainly worth a shot.

They also wondered, Why white chocolate? Why now? Their body
never answered and they felt frustrated at their body for never
hankering after white chocolate when they drove past the minimarts
on their way home. Often they would stop at a minimart anyway
and march their body up and down the aisles, perusing every shelf,
every need, every desire, counting every second, every minute,
waiting for the white chocolate craving to make its appearance.

But it never did. Not there.

They would have to return to their room
before the physical craving set in.

They would always shake their head in frustration. They felt
they didn't know their body anymore. It was a stranger
enshrouded in mist.

And yet what was happening to their body was clear enough:
unconsciously, they were remembering their first date with you—
back when you still wanted them—for, consciously, they had tried
to forget that night entirely. They had gone to the salon to fix
their hair, nails, and face; to the café to feel less lonely and to read
their favourite books; to the dental clinic to see their favourite dentist
and make love, and make love, and make love, before returning
to their room, turning off the light, thinking about their mother
and father who were no more, and crying themself to sleep.
In the morning, they would feel strangely refreshed, and think,
I've moved on! I'm ready! I've turned over a new leaf! And then
they'd get ready for work. They'd dive into a sea of documents
and tasks, dive into a sea of books and coffee, dive into a sea of their
dentist's hot steamy breath on their neck. And yet everything
about that night, from when you offered them white chocolate
and poured them wine, to when you read them poems
by Wisława Szymborska, to the very sweetness of that chocolate
on their tongue and in their soul, had already transformed
into tens, hundreds, thousands, millions of beta-actin proteins
incubating in the seahorse in their brain. They had no idea
that what was happening these days, what they were doing
these days, were the lingering effects of that night's enchantment.

They felt they'd forgotten and moved on.
Their body on the other hand remembered and stayed put.

And so body and soul began to diverge on the sly.

One morning when they emerged from the shower, they discovered
their self eyeing themself askance. Have I done something
wrong? they snapped. *Don't look at me like that!* they wanted
to say, but what their lips uttered instead was, 'Stop moping.'

Moping? What do you mean? Their body's behaviour
was most disturbing.

Day by day, it grew worse.

At the supermarket they discovered a can of their body's favourite pork
luncheon meat in their shopping cart. They stood at the till frozen
to the spot. When did I put this here? they thought. And why
did I put this here? What was I thinking? Didn't I swear off meat
just two days ago? And haven't I always wanted deep down
to give up meat? Why does everything I do take me farther
away from what I actually want? What's wrong with me?
Abandoning their cart at the counter without paying, they fled
to their car in the parking lot and cried for a very long time.
The cashier came after them. They went back inside
and paid for their items. They never went back to that supermarket
again and now take a more roundabout route to work.

And that is why, sometimes, when they are back home and their body
demands a bar of white chocolate, they strip their body naked and
extinguish the lights and lie face up on their bed and grope for the
air-conditioner remote and when they find it, turn the temperature of
their room down to 16°C, so their body can feel what they feel
every day, so their body will stop blaming them for every pang
of grief it deems excessive, so their body will understand
why they've gone through everything that they've gone through
and all they haven't gone through and all they'll never go through—
so their body will understand that these feelings are perfectly normal,
endured by every soul within every human being.

You see how it feels, they say, to their freezing breasts,
to their chattering teeth, to their shivering shoulders.
Why don't you see how I feel every day?

And you show me how to be happy.

LA VITA NUOVA

His father wanted to give new life
to the barren fig tree out back.

His father told him to pluck
a ripe fruit from the Tree of Life.

His father hurled the fruit earthward and squashed it underfoot
—exactly as he would someday crush the serpent's head.

His father retrieved the fruit and smeared
it around the fig tree's trunk.

His father said: Let it mutate and let the worms translate it
into a tongue spoken by trees

At that moment, his eyes were opened
and the world was no longer mysterious.

The new mayor built an imaginary park
in the heart of the city. We can all see it
from the latticed windows in our tiny rooms:
the giant iron gates, the brick-paved paths,
the grove of pines, the grassy lawns
dotted with all kinds of flowers,
the small lake in the northeast corner
complete with swan boats and
algae floating in the shallows
and ducks and their little sign too:
'Warning: Don't Feed the Ducks'.
In the lake swim the mujairs
and in the mothers' mouths swim their kids.
We don't eat the mothers, the mothers don't eat the kids.
The lake gives it all a nice blue touch.
The grass gives it all a nice green touch.
The fireflies offer themselves as lights.
Every night. We set up a big screen.
Men and women come to watch movies
about themselves, filmed with hidden cameras.
The street lamps glow, the moonlight
shimmers across the lake. The rain falls.
The water seeps between the bricks,
deep into the earth to the river beneath.
All the waria in the city work there.
Male-to-females as gardeners and street sweepers,
security guards, vets, and arborists,
landscape architects and accountants,
recreation managers and lifeguards too—
ready to dive in after anyone
who can't figure out how to get back
to land. They'll never go hungry again,

never have to wait for the cars
that slow, then stop. Every full moon,
a magical unicorn leaps out from
behind the curtain of pines—
shining like the North Star—
showering blessings on the park,
showering blessings on the city.
Another hard day over and
before we turn in, we all dream
about that park the mayor made
just for us. We feel better.
We feel better.

FOOTNOTE TO 33

I was just about to trim the wick of my lamp
when they showed up on that donkey of theirs.

An island drifted in those eyes—a dead one,
not a single dock in sight. They seemed to me
to be sailing solo in a storm, trying to flee
that island. Then without so much as a hello,
they asked me about the address scrawled
on the scrap of paper in their hand.

I pointed
down an unbending road
ending in the valley of wolves,
where that old snake lives—
in the tree of death
encircled by the bones of ten thousand sheep.

I thrust the lamp at them.
Take this
so you don't get lost.
They nodded,
then started down the road.

They'll never reach their destination
the mountain
where you live alone,

waiting for me to come home.

You see, I had to lead them astray
so they and I would
run into each other again.

HAPPY IDEA

> *I had the happy idea to polish the reflecting glass and say*
> *hello to my own blue soul.* Hello, blue soul. Hello.
> *It was my happiest idea.*

— Mary Szybist

He has the happy idea
to place an *i*
at the head
of a line
about God
so *I* too
will begin
tall

capital

equal

peering
for once
into the face
of the One
he loves
and holding Them
by the hand:

each quietly
studying
the other.

AUBADE

we are the flowers you don't
want us to be.

—Wiji Thukul, 'Flowers and Walls'

You've been here since five a.m., gathered at this McDonald's.
    Last night you watched
Prayers for Bobby, and at the part where Mary sobbed
to the pastor about her son committing suicide,   Panji cracked up
saying   *Tony's crying!*   and you all cracked up too
even as secretly   under cover of darkness   you each wiped away tears.

The night's dregs are spent   in idle chatter
    about the long shadows cast by parents
        and that dream eternal of moving to the Netherlands
    (though you know it'll never happen) until
        you're all famished. Two years ago

Tony came out   to his parents,   and hasn't been home
since.   He called his mother at her office.
She sobbed, 'Tony come home.   Don't be scared.
Mommy will take you to Doctor Frankie,'—as if *I'm attracted*
to men   is like having diarrhoea. How many
of you   sat mute   in the back of the car   as your parents

sneered

at the waria singing in the streets.   Now you're snickering—
hey hey how funny would it be   if Tony's parents   ran into him
in heaven one day   and died a second time?

Heaven,
 Tony?
  Yeah right

Silence falls and it dawns on you that everything
    is fading away:
the floors, the plates, the tables and chairs, the puddles
of ice cream... The sun out of nowhere is high above
 the trees, the green grass, the field of concrete, the Camry
Fiqar can't afford, the hibiscus buds unprepared
to burst into bloom, the stone wall separating rich
from poor, male from female, separating your kind
from the rest of the world. It's a new day,
 and fear is far behind. You know
life doesn't stop here. There will be no Bobby

no more

LIVES IN ACCRUAL ACCOUNTING, YOURS AND MINE

If we take life experience to be a form of Revenue,
then we must count every hardship we encounter
as an Expense, and by terming hardships Expenses
we cease being vague about them and feel compelled
instead to assess which hardships are the direct result
of our everyday activities, Operating Expenses we'll term them,
and which ones aren't—let's call these Miscellaneous Expenses—
and which hardships, over several years' time, will trigger
yet more 'experiences', and should therefore be counted
as Assets; once we measure the utility of the hardships
aforementioned we must then estimate how many years we
can derive benefit from them (for example, experiencing our first
breakup will undoubtedly help us prepare for our second one
and so on and so forth) as well as what Residual Value will
remain once these hardships have ceased to be of further use;
the initial value of each hardship will gradually depreciate over
a several-year period until it becomes an Expense,
and we must assess the most suitable method of calculating
our per annum Expenses, one that most closely approximates
how our lives operate and then maybe we can spread these Expenses
out across the entire sum of our years, or—if we hold that the finest
experiences are to be gained from hardships that are still fresh
in one's mind, *ceteris paribus*—apply the double-declining-balance
method so the annual depreciation of each hardship's value
as an Asset diminishes and diminishes and diminishes…
before it finally arrives at its Residual Value.

Once all Revenue and Operating Expenses are accounted for, we
can line them up side by side to arrive at our Annual Gross Profit
(or Loss), and after subtracting this sum, along with
Miscellaneous Expenses, we can calculate our Net Profit (or Loss);

naturally, if we make a profit, we must pay tax, surrendering a portion
of what we receive to the Government as a means of redistributing
our life experience in the hope that social equity will
ensue—social equity, meaning that the wealth of experience
will circulate beyond select individuals, so that one's
inherited privilege won't play a more significant role
than hard work in determining someone's success—
though it's a shame that our Net Profit has to undergo
a fiscal correction because of how Revenue and Expenses
are calculated for the purposes of accounting and taxes. But
this doesn't mean we labour in vain. It means we labour
in the hope of perfection…

Adi, I've checked around the shoe piles near the door and
there's still no letter from you: not one—single, soggy,
rain-drenched. I've turned my head at the lane's end
and found not even the faintest glimmer
of your face, smiling, your lips
exactly those of your father's.
I woke up and found a bald heart beating
I was lying in brown water, surrounded by leaves
I saw the fog herding them off
to the old church they shuttered for good.
Did we watch it on the news?
Do we remember so we can forgive ourselves
when we forget?
I opened the refrigerator
and its winter was like a rope you held onto, Dek—
under us, the abyss waving and waving
—and you cut it
when you were ready
to go, but I still long to be here.
(Has the school taught you past tense? And
the word winter, the word spring?)
I still love an air-conditioned library
I still love a sandwich crust
both of which you always hated
and lend me your ear: I now have a boyfriend no one knows about
I always thought of a murmur in the wind as a non-metaphor
but I am just your blue older brother

I tried soft-shoeing in your footsteps in the house, in my room
thinking if I stopped making stupid mistakes, I could
find some hidden drawing—some uglier but more beautiful version
of [ ]
but the floor is embarrassingly dirt-white
and oh the train to Christmasland is
chugging off again.

FINDING LEO

/

He is still unaware, as he climbs the stairs
and peers through the glass door, that the figure in white

is his Leo.

He's twenty-four and writes love letters
for himself to read.

He doesn't know what lies post-door,
that he'll finally have the right to call his life 'life.'

No more storing up loose change in heaven
yearning for his time on earth to end.

A FLYER

This software will assemble a series of steps that
will guarantee you'll be happy for the rest of your life.

It was created in response to skewed notions of 'happiness'
which have caused acute sorrow of pandemic proportions.

To begin, please enter your personal data, including
your *real* taxable income and passwords. All of your passwords.

The programme will compile news stories, laws, cultural norms,
and noteworthy social media posts relevant to your current location.

Using the information amassed, it will generate a SWOT matrix
to keep as a basis for further assessment, at which point,

under the software's guidance, you will ascertain what you must do
to exploit your strengths, combat weaknesses, seize opportunities,

and anticipate threats, thus providing you with financial, familial,
legal, social, and spiritual fulfilment and security.

Of course, if your tastes and preferences are somewhat unique—
let's say you're a lesbian who has a love

for cats and classic poems
like *Inferno* or *Paradise Lost*—more time will be required

to complete the mapping process (solvable
by upgrading your computer's RAM to 16 GB). Also,

the programme may need to ask further questions: Is it essential for you to be with someone who loves reading too?

Are you prepared to compromise when it comes to your sexuality—would you be willing to make out with a man in the dark?

Have you saved enough, are you brave enough to start life afresh in a place better able to accommodate you:

Antarctica, for instance?

This software also takes other users' priorities into account. For example, if 200 would-be college applicants are obsessed

with getting a certain degree at the most prestigious university in Country X and there are only 150 spaces, then the programme

will be forced to advise the 50 users with the lowest academic scores to settle. Failure is a punch in the guts

and they have to face facts. You would derive maximum benefit if your nearest and dearest signed up:

accounting for environmental factors
will produce more accurate results.

You see, we believe that an individual's path to happiness is coextensive with the paths of others

and is sometimes even at cross-purposes—
like a trawl net.

However, if you come across this flyer only after everyone else is dead: Even better. You can use the programme straight   away.

SEEKING ANOTHER EARTH
(YOUR PRE-AESCHYLEAN PLAY
IN THREE ACTS)

ONE

Voices report
that you are
in a black pond
carpeted with stars
so you dream that
you are in a black
pond carpeted with stars
and the spying eyes
that circle you
dream in a black pond
carpeted with stars

a girl has been set adrift
all on her own.

You are on a mission
to rescue your beloved.
She left on an earlier wave
and your plan was to wait for her,
to play the granny she never had,
but the station on Jupiter
received word that a comet swerved
into their ship: they're safe,
but the vessel is beyond all repair.
Now you want out of this sorry script,
and not just 'cause every light bulb is fried
and the speakers are on the fritz.
The other kids have stopped showing up—
your ship burst into flames and not
a single technician was around.
At least you're unfettered—your drama teacher
fled the scene after emitting a shriek of despair.

Voices report
that you're racking your brains,
seeking an emergency exit—
No messiah!
No messiah for you!
All them friends are Judases!
—so you dream that you're
racking your brains,
seeking an emergency exit,
as the spying eyes that circle you
dream there is an emergency exit,
that you're racking your brains,
that what they see is merely
the shell of something majestic
and intricate, that will leap out
from behind the curtain
any moment now.

'We can't film live anymore,' says the executive producer. 'We'll finish
the entire next season in a three-week-long shooting marathon.'
The director blanks out. She'll be meeting her son later that night,
as her ex-wife waits outside in their old car. Maybe she can get
a cheaper present. Maybe the 7 inch tablet will do instead of
the 9 inch. How do you make a farewell dinner memorable for a kid
who's blocked you on Facebook when, technically, you've just lost
your job and been stripped of any glory you've had in the world
of television: *Everyone, feel free to wing it—this night belongs to you.*

This whole damn life is *live*, thinks the director, and it's not like she's
ever received any cues from *her* director—if she even has one. She feels
like she has to find a perpetual balance between being a wild horse
running around in the woods and spending her life in a cage,
sustained by a water bottle and wilted produce from the market.
And then there's the fact that she keeps screwing up her own show.
'What kind of bleeping god are you, leaving me to bleep around
in this bleeping world?' The audience gapes and stares.
But there's only one channel—it's fixed.

CHANGE

Even after the screen has faded to black,
and it's

                                        'Seven years later...'

their ankle still aches
at the approach of
rain. They recall how it began:
when they slipped on the pavement
outside Ratu Plaza,
and hobbling had to hurry
after their bus

and no Simone of Cyrene
was with them to hold their hand.

Their mum died making pancakes—the green flying saucer ones he loved. He and his sister found her body sprawled on the kitchen floor. She was warm still, though there was no heartbeat. He sprinted next door screaming for help. The neighbours loaded her into their car and they all rushed to the hospital. Briefly she came back to life. Told him and his sister to love one another. *Now Mother Mary's your mum and Jesus your dad.* He sobbed. *How can a mum and kid be a mum and dad?* She ran out of breath before supplying an answer. The two kids sat in the hospital hallway and cried. It was past noon when they got home. At the dining table was their littlest brother. He had been asleep when they'd left. Nothing remained of the pancakes. He had wolfed the whole half-batch down. 'Serves you right for leaving me behind,' he said. 'Where's Mum? You all went out for ice cream, didn't you?'

ON A PAIR OF YOUNG MEN IN THE UNDERGROUND CAR PARK AT FX SUDIRMAN MALL

Is there anything more moving than two young men
in a Toyota Rush parked in the corner of level P3,
stealing a little time and space for themselves,
exchanging kisses wide-eyed—keeping watch as one
for security guards or janitors, in each other's arms,
escaping the loneliness of another week living
someone else's life. A friend dismissed
their feelings as *unnatural urges*
but each of them knows who he is now. Both
are sure the longing they feel is genuine *longing*
and the love in their hearts is the same *love* that made
Sergius and Bacchus one, and the loneliness they feel in their vacant rooms
is no different from John Henry Newman's from 1876 to his death,
and isn't it this world that has everything wrong,
that has no clue about who they are?
As Aelred of Rievaulx said, there is nothing more exquisite
than to love and be loved, which is true even though
they know also *the world isn't ready for us.*
It baffled Thérèse of Lisieux to see God playing favourites,
why blessings weren't doled out in equal amounts
to each soul, why a sinner like Augustine of Hippo
got to wear a white robe, all shimmering and spotless.
The two young men even wondered sometimes
why they were the ones who had to show love
can bloom anywhere, even in the dark,
and that love growing in the dark is no less life-giving.

Here we are in the garden again.

He used to boast of his handiwork—the blue sky,
the morning milkman passing by,
the mailman who never stops,
the urchins racing pigeons with the setting sun,
the police dog's bark in the quiet night.
He made it all. From none.

    'Must we live apart like this?' I ask.

No answer. Not even
the usual long-winded reply.

    'It's unbearable. You. Me. This.'

I recall his old line about unrequited love,
how he bore it for thousands of years,
the messengers he sent and they stoned,
how up on his mountain, it was he who was alone.

My foot is asleep. Still no answer.

    'Who were you writing to, anyway, up on the mountain?'

Still no answer.

Still no answer.

Still no answer.

Still no answer.

Still no answer.

This sky could be bluer.

TERMINATION LETTER

Imagine her surprise that morning
when she opened her desk drawer and discovered the envelope:

To [insert her name], it read, *From* [insert her name again], and inside
was a letter written in her own hand (utterly identical,
from the shape of each *e* to the diacritic-like dot above every *i* and *j*)
and also a list of the questions that had stumped her
during her performance review last week,
complete with a few pieces of advice, one of them being
Don't go out with Danny, which gave her cause for a little leap
because it was already too late and they'd made plans to see each other again.
See you at the top! it said by way of conclusion.

Sitting in her cubicle, she turned to stone,
racking her brain about how to lodge a complaint
about this woefully belated attempt at assistance
while drawing a blank on necessary details like:
Who do we end up with? Are we rich? Can we afford to be buried here in Jakarta?

Later, that evening, rummaging through her purse for loose change,
she discovered yet another envelope, sent by two people this time:
[insert her name] and [insert her name],
the second iteration crayoned in turquoise blue.
On the bus, standing wedged among all the people,
she went stone-still, a brief missive in her hand stating
that after observing her performance over the past week,
we both (how odd, she thought) *have made the executive decision to:*

(1) *discontinue you as the past*
(2) *discontinue you as the future.*

Was this for real? If so, how egotistical,
how misogynistic could her pre- and post-selves get?
The nerve they had, erasing her from the history of [insert her name]!
As she watched her fellow passengers dozing off, clutching
their respective poles, tears trickled down her cheeks.
From now on she was on her own.

THEOPHILUS

'It's too dark. I can't see.'

> Let there be light, the Friend whispered.
> And then there was light. The man scampered around
> the green grounds on his chubby legs all day.

'The sun's so strong. I'm parched.'

> Let there be water. And then there was water.
> The young man knelt by the bank,
> cupped his hands together and drank.

'A charming island. But so far away.'

> Let there be creatures of all kinds. Horses.
> Lions and tigers. Birds in the air. The man
> walked up to a donkey and saddled himself on its back.

'It's so deserted. I'm lonely.'

> The Friend was silent.

> *You will never be with the someone who loves you most.*

'Let there be someone else,' said the Friend.
And then there he was, a someone else—like the man.

Some nights his eyes fly open at the thought of you in bed, and he
wonders whether you're lying there asleep or wide awake. When you
sit facing each other on that five a.m. commute, knees grazing knees
with each jostle of the koasi, there are no circles under your eyes.
Some nights when his eyes fly open, as he wonders if you're asleep
or awake, he's positive you must be awake, although every day
at five a.m., amidst the mingling aromas of cheap fabric sprays
used to iron work clothes the night before, there are never
any dark circles underneath your eyes. And some nights
when he's positive you must be awake, although you never have circles
under your eyes whenever you sit face to face on that five a.m.
commute, your fellow passengers trying to hit play on dreams
put on pause by morning showers, he imagines himself reading you
a poem by Szymborska out loud. You don't seem like the poetry-liking
type, but maybe he could be the poetry-liking type who likes people
who don't like poetry, after all your knees brush against each other
every morning, riding the five-in-the-morning koasi, everyone's spying
eyes window-ward, searching desperately for the dream derailed
by a gayung full of cold water, and maybe you could be the type
who likes listening to a person who likes both poetry and people
who don't like poetry reading Syzmborska's poetry to you out loud,
because you don't seem like the type to get hung up on minor things
and also, you're all too aware that not preferring something doesn't
mean you can't stand it, so you won't mind listening to someone
who likes both poetry and people who don't like poetry read
Szymborka's poetry to you. After all, he's reading it for you. After all
his knees graze yours every morning at five in the morning,
in that koasi, cheerful with its orange hue, your face from last night
washed away in the water pouring from the gayung, after all
whether or not the poem even exists, whether or not there's a poet
named Szymborska, whether or not there's a person who likes both
poetry and people who don't like poetry doesn't matter to you.

The koasi will trundle on until its terminus at Setia Kawan. You'll
carry on with life from there on your non-air-conditioned bus
to Jakarta, with the windows open. And every night

you'll drift back
    to sleep
        without hearing him
            read you that Szymborska poem at all.

in his room on the fourth floor he hears a knock on the window,
twice, three times. *Open up,* the man says
though he's been gone for years and years,
so I can come in. He's midway through the fourth line
and absolutely sure this time
at long last
poetry will save his life.
You never think about me, do you?
He nods, but after this poem
I can crumble and live utterly alone.

CURRICULUM VITAE ₂₀₁₅

The world I lived in had a soft voice and no claws.
—Lisel Mueller

1) Three months before he was born the Romanian dictator and his wife were executed before a firing squad. To this day his mother still talks about it.

2) When he was little he fell from a tree. Ever since, his first memory of his father was himself in school uniform, squatting on the toilet. This stemmed from his first day of school—he was five and right before they set off he told his father he needed to poop.

3) The first thing he learned at school, as he watched the girls during break, was that there was a girl inside him. He believed that when he grew up his penis would expire and his breasts would sprout.

4) He didn't say much and only learned to read when he was finishing second grade. In front of a friend of his mother's, the mother of one of his friends dubbed him 'the stupid one'. His mother's friend told his mother and when he was grown up, his mother told him.

5) He was awful at making friends and spent most of his time reading or playing Nintendo and Sega. The first book he read was a book of Japanese folktales.

6) Some of the neighbours forbade their kids from playing with him and his brothers because his family was Batak and Christian.

7) He had no friends and didn't realise how sad this was.

8) His father punished him with beatings. One day he eavesdropped on his parents—his father was worried because according to him their firstborn son acted like a girl. He peered into the mirror, to the little girl inside. And he saw it was good.

9) Once his father kicked him—and sprained his ankle. His father had to take a day off work. His mother said all the trouble in their house flowed from him.

10) One Sunday morning, his father took him and his brothers to jog and play soccer on a badminton court nearby. *You banci!* his father screamed in front of everyone.

11) He accepted that he was a mistake. His first suicide attempt occurred the day before he started middle school.

12) He made it into the best high school in the city— where the government officials sent their kids. His only friend from middle school started avoiding him. The bud of loneliness blossomed into first love.

13) Not long after he graduated from college, he discovered the rest of the Batak community called him 'si banci' behind his back.

14) When he was twenty-two depression hit. One night his mind went entirely blank. His brother found him sitting in a stupor at a gas station by a mall.

15) He ran away. In a bookstore in Jakarta he discovered a book by Herta Müller. Herta wrote about Ceaușescu's Securitate. It reminded him of his mother. He read every English translation of her work and loved them all.

16) As he approached his twenty-third birthday, for some reason
he felt that he was male. And he saw it wasn't bad.

17) He moved back in with his parents.

18) He went back to work and began writing again.
In a novel-writing class he met you, the man who loves him.

19) To marry his mother, his father had sold a motorbike
he'd been leasing from his employer. He hopes to use
the royalties from his books to marry you.

20) He will grow old. You will grow old. Together you both will grow
old, and be wed before the Three-Branched God—the tree-like god—
and have a child named Langit. Your descendants will fill the Earth
so that whenever anyone is walking alone in the dark they will hear
from every window in every building on both sides of the street,
voices reaching out, 'Salam!' 'Salam!' 'Salam!'

A HISTORY-TO-COME OF HELMBRELLAS:
THEIR FEATURES AND FATES

I.

The following happened
to your granddaughter, long
after you opted
for euthanasia
—like the others.
She was still in high school
when it all began.
She watched as the spaceships parted the clouds,
how through their doors
emerged purplish black blobs
that shifted, and stirred,
and let loose a battle cry
like the croaking of frogs and the cawing of crows.
The Ulxians (that was the
term used thereafter) struck.
But the good people of Earth
prevailed in the end.

The alien bodies—
85% H2O, scientists said—
littered the earth.
The day after the victory
she saw the sun's steady rise.
With each putrid heap
that vanished
a cloud congealed overhead.
The sky turned pitch black.

And then it began to rain.

2.

Then your granddaughter observed
how fickle the weather turned.
Once it rained for a whole month,
setting the campus abuzz with whispers.

'Tis da Sixth Extinction, her friends said.
She was in her room when she heard
on the radio: the shantytowns in Mumbai swept away,
killing hundreds.

New drains and reservoirs
mushroomed throughout the city. New brands
of disposable umbrellas and raincoats flooded the market
—Ztormz, Water-Zip, Kaza, et cetera.

Her co-workers blew their bonuses on
buying these companies' shares.
She noticed everyone
in the city bringing umbrellas

or raincoats
wherever they went,
even on the sunniest days,
and she watched herself turn

into one of them.

3.

When the following trends transpired,
nobody was that surprised.

4.

The very first model,
the one that really
started it all,
was, naturally,
the plasma shield.
It was hardly original,
just recycled:
leftover
technology
from warring
with the Ulxians.

The military
made use
of handheld devices
that erected
plasma domes
to keep the Ulxians
from invading their bodies.
They generated
a wave
that would attract polymer
fragments
from the atmosphere,
turning

the air into plasma.

5.

Those with relatives in the army were the first pioneers.
They procured the devices from their husbands/wives/children—
or from the uniforms that came with the bodies of the deceased.
They'd then mill around downtown or along Fifth Avenue,
like air bubbles with legs. The rain
   trickled
down
the domes'
invisible curves,
catching everyone's eye.

Hey now, dat'z some idea!
thought one onlooker, then two, then ten.
News sites caught whiff of the phenomenon.
'Sheer poetry!' proclaimed the *New York Times*.
The devices popped up on the black market overnight—
sold not as artefacts, like old Civil War relics,
but as everyday household items.
Megaconglomerates began lobbying the military,
eager to exploit the plasma shield.

6.

In reality,
the plasma shield
wasn't appropriate
for use in crowds,
and certainly
not on sidewalks.
If there was a sudden downpour,
people who were squeamish
about getting the least bit wet
would hastily activate
their devices,
and the expanding shield
would injure
people
in the vicinity.

The most horrifying incident
made the front page
on almost
all
the news sites:

three shields were activated simultaneously,
colliding and knocking over their users.
The resulting domino effect felled
fifteen others. One victim slammed into a steel bollard.
    He died
instantly from severe brain injuries.

7.

Governments the world over
banned the use of plasma shields.
This met with online petitions
and small-scale demonstrations
in front of city halls
in various states.

General Electric's
R&D Division
seized their chance.
In less than six months
they released
an alternative product,
a helmet-umbrella,
a helmbrella,
that generated
an anti-gravity field.
It worked by momentarily
suspending the raindrops
falling
on the wearer's head,
which would recommence
falling
once the wearer
was out of reach.
This model
also quickly
fell
out of popularity.

Think about it: if rain accumulating above someone
resumes descent, where does it fall?
    To earth.
By then who would be walking around on said earth?
    Someone else.

8.

Other, newer
models rapidly
became publicly
available.
Unlike when you
or your father were small,
the helmbrella a person used
defined who they were
inside.

9.

Not long after the
anti-gravity
model came out,

an electrolysis-
powered helmbrella
was released
and distributed
far and wide,
reaching even
the minimarts
way out in the sticks.

The helmbrella
generated
two electromagnetic
waves
that functioned
as an anode and cathode,
splitting the water molecules
into hydrogen and oxygen gas.

This was the first model
to demonstrate stability
under a wide range of
conditions.
And so subsequent helmbrellas
were created in the image of this godly
opus.
The only thing was
the induction process
would sprinkle the user
with grains of salt

which were easily
mistaken for dandruff.
But this was so trivial
that this model is still in use today.

10.

A few people took
the fever too far.
Take the Star Wars fans—the last of their kind.
In conjunction with Honda, they launched
a model made up of miniature X-wings
which circled above their masters' heads,
shooting laser beams,
incinerating raindrops
at light speed.

This model never caught on.
Obviously, it was cumbersome
and not energy-efficient,
but it did find its niche—
people who wanted to stand out.
Avant-garde designers began to create
all sorts of new models.
For instance,
a helmbrella comprising
swarming mechanical
fireflies, hot to the touch
    (thereby evaporating every
raindrop on contact).
It debuted at Paris Fashion Week.

II.

The Potterheads, who
by some miracle survived
into this era,
tried to make the Impervius charm
a reality. They attempted to invent a water-deflection device
that would produce the same effect
as two magnetic poles of like polarity.
Their efforts have never seen the light of day.

12.

Wondrous news from Jepara, in small-town Indonesia:
a middle-schooler, a loner and film buff
who worshipped Christopher Nolan
built his own: a helmbrella topped with a spike
that functioned as wormhole generator.

The rain would fall
straight into the wormhole
and out the other side,
through the corresponding generator
and into a gutter.

The teen prodigy
was whisked away on a whirlwind
tour of the US. He appeared on:

The Late Night Show

Today's Science

Hello America

The New, New Thing

But he got depressed,
overwhelmed
by the popularity and offers
from companies that poured in nonstop.
He became a recluse.

13.

The most bizarre model
in recorded history
came from
some religious types. One of those

New New New Age sects.

They bought up all the remaining
anti-gravity helmbrellas.
and did a complete overhaul.

They attached shiny metal orbs that spouted
fire to the top of the helmbrellas.
Naturally, when switched on
the fireballs seemed to hover
above the wearers' heads.

They baptised it the Holy Spirit Helmbrella.

This design was ineffective in the extreme,
considering it couldn't handle
all the rain falling on the wearer.
Plus, whenever it poured,
the fire would get snuffed out in places,
giving the ball bald spots.

The other problem was
that if the helmet broke
or a powerful sneeze
caused the user's head
to tilt forward.
The ball sometimes slid
off onto the user,
and even if the anti-gravity field
made a split-second save
it would sometimes hurl the ball at bystanders.

Surprisingly, its sales were pretty good.
People wore it to be ironic. There were two hundred
reported cases of wearers, three-quarters of them men,
suffering brain damage because of this model.

14.

No one knows
if this craze
will continue,
    or if it lasts, how long,
    and where it will head,
but one thing is clear: Earth's remaining inhabitants,
a mere quarter of the pre-Ulxian-invasion population,
have found a new hobby,
after spending
so many centuries
being fed
up with everything:

in the end,

there is nothing new under the sun,

much less under the shade of a tree. Or an armpit.

15.

And the model
that is the classic-of-classics?
The conical, elongated cane
that opens and shut
when taken out and put away,
which you brought everywhere,
well into your fifties, even when
taking your granddaughter
to the zoo for the first time?
No one uses it.

'Tis hopelezzly archaic, everyone says.
What's nostalgia in the face of practicality?
But you know something?
Your granddaughter still picks it up sometimes,
when she misses you or her mother.
She and her wife
brave the rain, hand in hand,
to visit their favourite used bookshop or café,
and she talks about the two of you.
And not a single passer-by

stares.

'Poetry': The lyrics 'Laos dilanglangi do ahu, tarlungun-lungun' were taken from the Batak pop song 'Mardalan Ahu'. The song was originally written by Tilhang Gultom and was popularised by several Batak singers, including Korem Sihombing and Vicky Sianipar. This poem is after Morri Creech.

'Cooking Instant Noodles at the End of the Rainbow': 'There's nothing at the end of the rainbow. There's nothing to grow up for anymore.' —Richard Thompson

'What the Dead Ask from the Departed' is for Lobsang Tenphel.

'La vita nuova': 'I'm sorry. We know how it works. The world is no longer mysterious.' —Richard Siken

'ROMCOM': 'From now on, you write and shoot the whole season in two weeks like *Wheel of Fortune* or FOX News.' —Jack Donaghy, *30 Rock*

'Termination Letter' is for Swistien Kustantyana.

'A History-to-Come of Helmbrellas: Their Features and Fates' is for Ninus D. Andarnuswari.

BEYOND THE BINARY—
A NOTE ON TRANSLATING

PROCESS

It is difficult to express the extent to which working with Norman Erikson Pasaribu on this translation has been a transformative experience. (Perhaps hardly surprising since the *trans*—'across'—of *translate* and *transform* is one and the same.) I was unsure of my abilities when it came to poetry and very grateful at how involved in the process Norman was willing to be. We ended up working so closely together that I feel the binary labels of 'translator' and 'author'— i.e. translator *or* author, translator *not* author—ring somewhat false. They imply our roles in bringing about the English edition of *Sergius Seeks Bacchus* were separate when, in reality, they were mingled and merged.

There was no one method we used; it depended on the poem. Sometimes, I would produce a draft translation based on the original poem and then from there, Norman and I would exchange edits and suggestions. Sometimes, Norman would tweak the original Indonesian version for me to translate in order to achieve a certain effect he wanted for the English version. In a few cases, Norman had created his own translations of the poems prior to working with me, and I would refer to these in order to create my own. For 'Happy Idea' and 'Are You Still There at the Station', Norman created new English versions based on my translations, which we then edited together. There were times I listened to audio recordings of him reading the poems so I could better internalize the tone and rhythm he sought for each one. Often, we would think we were finally satisfied with a poem, only to revisit it later and decide it needed either drastic alterations or more fine-tuning. Always, I relied a great deal on the notes and personal experiences Norman would share with me in our online conversations, where the bud of literary partnership blossomed into fast friendship. And I depended constantly on Norman's encouragement to be daring—to be less literal, more poetic; less inhibited, more playful; less logical, more personal.

As we continued to work on the poems, continued to correspond, something else happened. I found Norman's words, my translations of Norman's words, and our conversations seeping into me, unsettling my self from myself, altering my thoughts, perspectives, opinions, and emotions. I already tend to be an empath when it comes to translating (I've likened it in other spaces to surrogate motherhood or spirit-channelling), but sometimes I would find myself reduced to tears or devastated by the sadder poems—as if by translating I were consuming their sorrow into myself; as if their sorrow was speaking to my own sorrow, coaxing it out of my bones. I also became more aware of the heteronormative assumptions and privilege on which so many of my thoughts and values rested. Honestly, I don't think I can ever go back to being the person I was before. I hope I don't.

Whenever I say I'm the translator of *Sergius Seeks Bacchus*, I always find myself elaborating what that role has meant in this context: the author and I have worked together so closely on these poems that 'translator' isn't the right word at all. What I really want to say is that I and Norman are the translator, not just I. And I also want to say that I feel as if I am more than just the 'translator' (in the narrow, prevalent sense of the word)—Norman's poems have become part of and spring from me as well.

PRONOUNS

The translation of this collection into the book you hold in your hands required a dismantling of the translator/author binary. But it also opened my eyes to the extent to which the English language has imposed limitations on my ability to think about gender in fluid, rather than binary, terms. English is the language I am most fluent in, although my parents and grandparents are Chinese-Indonesian. My parents spoke to me in English and sent me to English-medium schools, even in Jakarta where I lived for six years. Though I heard my parents and other relatives speak Indonesian and sometimes spoke it myself, it was only when I was in graduate school at UC Berkeley that I started to improve my Indonesian by taking language classes and reading Indonesian books.

Because English tends to be my default language, when I see the Indonesian third-person pronoun 'dia' I instinctively assign it a gender, translating it into 'she/her' or 'he/him'. I also do this for 'ia' (an alternate form of 'dia'), as well as the possessive '-nya' ('her'/his'). In reality, these pronouns are genderless: 'dia' could be a she or a he, a him or a her. The same with 'ia' and '-nya'. In this sense, these pronouns are akin to the English-language gender-neutral singular pronouns 'they'/'them'/'their'. But whereas with English, these pronouns are only just starting to be taken seriously and are (lamentably) sometimes criticised as invalid or ungrammatical, in Indonesian, the genderless pronouns are utterly conventional—the traditional norm.

So how did the gendered pronouns of English affect how I as a translator approached the genderless pronouns of Norman's poetry collection? It meant my brain assumed that every 'ia' and 'dia' was concealing whether someone was a 'she/her' or 'he/him'. And in poems where there were no indicators of whether the 'ia/dia' was a she or a he, I assumed it was necessary for me to find out which one they were and to translate accordingly—this in a collection about queerness and fluidity, much to my shame. Even worse, more often than not, I would assume that the 'ia' or 'dia' was a 'he'—thus exposing the extent to which I was translating with

a thoroughly colonised mind. Norman would issue gentle correc-
tions via WhatsApp. Mortified, I'd apologise. I began asking him
before I would start translating a poem whether an 'ia' or 'dia' was
male or female, not realising how utterly insufficient this still was
and that my thinking needed to be completely rewired. Finally, we
had a conversation where I commented that the English translations
of some of the poems were forcing them to 'come out' because
the gender of the 'ia/dia' was being made apparent. And then he
observed that since I grew up with English as a first language, I
tended to read some of the poems as straight because I was used to
all pronouns being gendered. Whereas to him, because 'dia' and 'ia'
were nonbinary, he saw the same poems as obviously queer.

It was clear prior to this conversation, but even more glaringly so
afterwards that without our close consultation and correspondence,
my translation would have run the very likely risk of reinforcing and
reproducing the heteronormative and binary narratives that *Sergius
Seeks Bacchus* was written to challenge. Norman was also responsi-
ble for suggesting a revision of the manuscript to translate various
instances of the third-person singular pronouns as the gender-neutral
'they', 'their', and 'them'. The results of this crucial intervention are
'Footnote to 33', 'Change', 'Update on the Left-Behind Woman',
as well as 'Happy Idea' in which, importantly, God is now no longer
a 'He' but a 'Them'. *But of course! Of course, 'the three-branched God—
the tree-like god—' is a Them!*

POLY-

People often talk about what is 'lost in translation'. Indeed, the phrase has become positively banal. But what about that which is wilfully or unconsciously erased in translation to simplify foreign writers and their writing in order to make them easily comprehensible for an English-reading audience?

Thinking beyond binaries means being able to process multiplicity. Norman is more than just a queer Indonesian poet. He is a queer Batak poet from Indonesia. He is a queer Toba-Batak poet from a working-class background from Indonesia. He is a queer Toba-Batak-Indonesian poet from a working-class Christian background. Please hold these simultaneously in your head. *Sergius Seeks Bacchus* is the confluence of them all. Queerness is not lived in a vacuum; it is mediated through culture, class, and belief.

'Poetry', which takes as its theme the heartache of a lifetime of silenced queerness, is articulated through a melancholy Batak-language pop song about self-imposed exile—the Batak tradition of leaving one's home to seek a livelihood elsewhere. In 'Erratum', the rejection the protagonist endures for coming out is also the ejection from his Toba-Batak home—a warm nest lined with specific cultural practices and traditions into which he was welcomed at birth with kisses and feasting and joy. In 'Curriculum Vitae 2015', being Batak (i.e. an ethnic minority; Bataks make up about 3.5% of Indonesia's population) and Christian (i.e. a religious minority in Indonesia) means that the queer protagonist is on the margins of the margins—out of place in his body and family, which in turn are out of place in the place they reside. There are also the markers of Batakness in names, words, speech patterns, and images throughout the poems that come across in English less clearly or not at all (for example, Christian images and terms, or references to the Bible and saints, because of the influence of Christianity on contemporary Batak culture).

If Batakness is an inalienable part of a queer Batak's identity, despite rejection from their Batak family and community, the same could be said of the relationship between Christianity and the queer person of Christian background. As the poems indicate, religious affiliation is not necessarily a matter of choice. Biblical stories and verses, religious traditions, theology, and history cannot be unwoven from the fabric of the mind and heart of someone raised Christian. But they can be reworked, reshaped, into new theologies—ones critical and questioning, ones hopeful and queer-affirming. New gospels for the queer community. Heavens where a Sergius and Bacchus can stroll the streets hand in hand in broad daylight, rather than confining their love to the subterranean carpark of a third-rate-and-therefore-relatively-deserted shopping mall. In this sense, the Christian dimension of many of the poems fulfils a function similar to the speculative dimension of poems like 'Seeking Another Earth […]' and 'A History-to-Come of Helmbrellas […]'. Queer individuals are loosed from the confining scripts written for queers by others, and set free in heaven, in a post-alien-invasion Earth, in outer space.

One also has to take class into account in order to understand *Sergius Seeks Bacchus*. The queer lives of Norman's poetry abide in the material world and have material needs. They have jobs that leave them exhausted at the end of each day and the start of the next. Their bodies live in rented rooms and boarding houses, with parents and with roommates. They lease cars they can't afford. They try to work out how to buy fancy tech they can't afford for their kids' birthdays. They commute by *koasi* all the way from Bekasi because it's too expensive to live in the city proper. The rich may not have to convert their life experiences and hardships into revenue and expenses, but those who operate on a slim margin (see 'Lives in Accrual Accounting, Yours and Mine') don't have much choice. Staying financially afloat is important because the price is high for being queer and poor. Respect, tolerance, and physical safety all require money. Ask Christy from 'Cooking Instant Noodles at the End of the Rainbow'. Ask the waria of the dystopic-but-also-factual 'Scenes from a Beautiful Life'.

PROCLAIM...

I hope that readers will recognise the miracle that this collection is, and the miracle that this translation is, and the miracle that Norman Erikson Pasaribu is, and the miracles that are the queer lives for whom these poems are a testament and a dedication. This is for all who walk alone in the dark, so they will hear from every window on every building on both sides of the street, voices reaching out, 'Salam!' 'Salam!' 'Salam!'

Tiffany Tsao

ACKNOWLEDGMENTS

The author and translator of this book want to thank the following journals for publishing poems from this book, sometimes in different forms or under different titles: 'He and the Tree', 'Sergius Seeks Bacchus', 'Inferno', 'Purgatorio', 'Paradiso', 'Curriculum Vitae' in *Asymptote*; 'Curriculum Vitae' and 'He and the Tree' were reprinted in AJAR; 'Cooking Instant Noodles at the End of the Rainbow' in *Cordite Poetry Review*; 'A History-to-Come of Helmbrellas: Their Features and Fates' in Asian American Writers' Workshop's *The Margins* for their Transpacific Literary Project; 'A Flyer' in *Modern Poetry in Translation*; 'On a Pair of Young Men in the Underground Car Park at fX Sudirman Mall', 'What the Dead Ask from the Departed', 'Scenes from a Beautiful Life', 'Update on the Left-Behind Woman' in *Asia Literary Review*. We would also like to thank English PEN for supporting and highlighting this book through their PEN Translates and PEN Presents programmes.

The author of this book also wants to send virtual hugs to Leopold Adi Surya, Mirna Yulistianti & Gramedia Pustaka Utama, Nhã Thuyên & Kaitlin Rees & the whole family of AJAR, Intan Paramaditha, Cyntha Hariadi, Ellen van Neerven, Saaro Umar, Han Yujoo, Gratiagusti Chananya Rompas, Naomi Srikandi, Sukutangan, and Perdana Putri.

ACKNOWLEDGMENTS

This edition published in the United Kingdom by Tilted Axis Press in 2019.
This translation was funded by Arts Council England.

This book has been selected to receive financial assistance from English
PEN's "PEN Translates" programme, supported by Arts Council England.
English PEN exists to promote literature and our understanding of it, to
uphold writers' freedoms around the world, to campaign against the perse-
cution and imprisonment of writers for stating their views, and to promote
the friendly co-operation of writers and the free exchange of ideas.
www.englishpen.org

tiltedaxispress.com

First published 2016 in Indonesian by Penerbit PT Gramedia Pustaka Utama
as *Sergius Mencari Bacchus*.

ISBN (paperback)   9781911284239
ISBN (ebook)   9781911284215

A catalogue record for this book is available from the British Library.

Edited by Theodora Danek and Emily Stewart
Cover design by Soraya Gilanni Viljoen
Typesetting and ebook production by Simon Collinson
Printed and bound by Clays Ltd, Elcograf S.p.A.

ABOUT TILTED AXIS PRESS

Founded in 2015 and based in London, Toronto, and Seoul, Tilted Axis is a not-for-profit press on a mission to shake up contemporary international literature.

Tilted Axis publishes the books that might not otherwise make it into English, for the very reasons that make them exciting to us – artistic originality, radical vision, the sense that here is something new.

Tilting the axis of world literature from the centre to the margins allows us to challenge that very division. These margins are spaces of compelling innovation, where multiple traditions spark new forms and translation plays a crucial role.

As part of carving out a new direction in the publishing industry, Tilted Axis is also dedicated to improving access. We're proud to pay our translators the proper rate, and to operate without unpaid interns.

We hope you find this fantastic book as thrilling and beguiling as we do, and if you do, we'd love to know.

tiltedaxispress.com

@TiltedAxisPress